P9-BZQ-244

ALASKA

ALASKA

BY ROBERT REYNOLDS
TEXT BY FR. JOHN J. MORRIS, S.J.

ALASKA

International Standard Book Number 0-912856-05-X
Library of Congress Catalog Card Number 77-155969

P.O. Box 10306 • Portland, Oregon 97210 • 503/224-7777
Designer • Robert Reynolds
Text • Fr. John J. Morris, S.J.
Typesetter • Paul O. Giesey/Adcrafters
Printer • Graphic Arts Center
Bindery • Lincoln & Allen
Printed in the United States of America
Ninth Printing

Right: Midday fog partially obscures supply laden barges making their way through Arctic ice floes near Plover Island east of Pt. Barrow. In August warm southeast winds melt frozen Arctic Ocean, letting waterborne cargo enter this area for a few weeks. Supplies are destined for oil exploration and DEW Line stations along north slope.

Below: Wide gravelled river bed below the north flank of the Alaskan Range in Mt. McKinley National Park. Unusual geological formations appear frequently in the Park area. *Right:* Slabs of ice form an interesting pattern on the surface of Wasilla Lake in the Matanuska Valley.

Below: View looking northwest from the Susitna River Valley in early evening, mighty Mt. McKinley dominates the horizon on the Alaskan Range. *Right:* Winter's generous mantle gracefully adorns a stand of cottonwood trees in the Chugach Mountain Range near Anchorage.

Below Ribbons of clouds line the coast mountains rising approximately 5,000 feet above the black water of the Lynn Canal north of Juneau. *Right:* Bog moss carpets the forest floor in the foothills of the Chugach Mountains near Copper Center on Richardson Highway.

Below: Matanuska River in early August. Viewed from Glenn Highway north of Palmer. Background, Chugach Mountains. *Right:* Light dusting of snow covers Matanuska Valley in early winter, at base of Chugach Range.

Below: A thick stand of birch trees lends brilliant contrast to mountains in Chugach Range near Birchwood. *Right:* Young birch tree heralds the coming of Spring on north slope of the Wrangell Mountains near Nabesna.

Below: Sun highlights red poppy along a roadside on Kenai Peninsula. Wild flowers abound in many areas.

TEXT BY FR. JOHN J. MORRIS S.J.

ALASKA'S FIRST PEOPLE

The low winter sun, as exotically beautiful and patronizing as the cruel goddesses of mythology, cast a soft pink hue over the treeless and terrifying expanse of the silent chilly arctic desert. I heard again the words of that wizened, old Eskimo woman at Kotlik, "If you wish to know the secret of Alaska's peoples stand at noon and peer strongly into the eye of the winter sun." I did as she had bidden.

The red ball, low and immense on the horizon, began to pulsate; my inner ear picked up the primitive beat of a skin drum. Within the orb a vision took place. I watched an ethereal vapor call to life thousands of years of history. An Asiatic people were moving from Siberia, out across the Kamchatka Peninsula, toward what we now call Alaska. The time I could not tell, but it was thousands of years ago. They were crossing a land bridge to the new continent, splitting into several streams as they progressed, some moving south, others north, and still others toward the interior. Along the way men and women were coveting, giving value, to such common, "useless" things as stones, grass, driftwood, bones, antlers, tusks. As if guided by some primeval wizard these fur-clad peoples were fashioning remarkable weapons, efficient tools, homes, and clothing out of almost nothing. Unbeknown to themselves they were creating an ingenious cultural pattern based on kinship with the spirits of the universe—the sky, water, earth, the animal, and fish—a cultural pattern which thousands of years later would tantalize technological man with its humaneness, endurance, simplicity, patience and cooperation.

Entranced, I watched these stalky people tame the wolf into a dog, create from their minds the sled, harpoon, and spear; squeeze from seal, walrus and fish, a fuel to give heat and light. In their great round faces I saw etched nobility and strength, gentleness and humanity. It was from this vision that I began searching the past to find their origins.

When the Russians touched Alaska in 1741 claiming it for the Tsar, and when the United States purchased it from the Russians in 1867, they both manifested an arrogance and naiveté beyond belief today. Neither party recognized that three separate and dignified races of people had inhabited that country for thousands of years, and that perhaps they might have something to say about it.

The Aleuts have, as is evidenced by their name, dwelt and developed along the twelve-hundred mile Aleutian Island chain. The Indians are of two main groups; the Athapaskan who dwell in the interior and extend far down into Canada's north country, and the Tlingit, who dwell along Alaska's panhandle. The Eskimos are a homogenous people extending from the Anchorage area, all along the Alaska coast (excepting the Aleutian Islands), up beyond Point Barrow, over across Canada to Greenland, making them the most widely-distributed, yet contiguous, race of people on earth.

Today the native population of Alaska is numbered at about 53,000, divided in the following manner: 52% are Eskimo, 34% are Indian, and 14% Aleut. But where did these people come from? Who is the Eskimo? How are the three different races related, or are they? Are there any established connections with the Indians of North and South America? Today, without speaking with utter certitude, social scientists do have some answers for us.

Sea charts indicate that if the present water level in the Bering Strait were to drop a little more than one hundred feet, we could walk to Russia with dry shoes. Yet, during the last Ice Age, called the Wisconsin glaciation, water was absorbed into mountains of ice to such an extent that the sea diminished almost three hundred feet in depth. The glaciation, however, was not one continuous process; it seems there were at least three different periods when the land bridge emerged only to be swamped again by warmer temperatures working on the glaciers. It would have been possible, and in fact archeological findings in our own Southwest as well as other places, lead scientists to speculate with some degree of surety that the first peoples migrated (it was, of course, an unplanned, imperceptible movement) before 40,000 years ago. Another crossing could have, and probably did, take place about 25,000 years ago. These are the ancestors of all Indians in North and South America, having in the meantime touched the tip of South America and practically every area of both continents.

It was during the last land bridge, nearly 12,000 years ago that the ancestors of the Eskimos crossed over, moving slowly along Alaska's coast, south to the Anchorage area and north to Canada, arriving in Greenland about 2,500 B.C.

Strange as it may seem, although during that period before 40,000 years ago, man could have both crossed over from Asia and migrated southward, during the later period (25,000 years ago), while there was a land bridge across, there was no corridor open toward Canada and the United States. It can be proven scientifically that although the Wisconsin glaciation went as far south as St. Louis, Missouri, covering most of the United States north of that, there was an ice-free corridor southward during that earliest period. It is therefore speculated, with the help of archeological finds in our southwest, western Canada, Alaska, and eastern Asia, that this migration was the source of Indians throughout the Americas.

Another interesting aspect of all this speculation is that the Alaskan Indians, instead of having come immediately across from Asia, are in all likelihood, a northward migration. From all discoveries in the panhandle area, it appears that the Tlingit are a rather recent arrival. We are not as certain about the interior Athapaskans.

The Aleut people display certain linguistic, anthropological and cultural features, which while relating these people to the Eskimos, still show them to be a people in their own right. It seems that the differentiation between Aleut and Eskimo began some 6,000 years ago. The Aleuts arrived at their present habitat by a migration from the mainland, probably down from the Alaska peninsula. It was along the 1,200 mile string of islands, the Aleutians, where these people stabilized and built a culture known today as Aleut.

While contact and acculturation has eroded some of the best and richest qualities of all these three races, the Aleuts more than the others felt the killing blows of "civilized" man. Being numerically the smallest group, and finding themselves directly in front of the Russian Bear's quest for furs, they were almost annihilated. All through the Russian period they were enslaved, pillaged, abused. Today there are fewer than 8,000 Aleuts, and most of them are of mixed blood of some degree. Study of their genuine, precontact culture is almost impossible.

ALASKA, LAND OF SUPERLATIVES

Sourdough Bill was sitting out on his small front porch, feet up on the log railing, rocking his chair on its two back legs, enjoying the warm, lazy day. I could see he was in a talking mood. "For the record, Bill," I paused for him to look up, "What is Alaska to you?"

"Shucks," he says, "that's a hard one. I've been up here so many years, seen so many different places, and read so many books that other fellas have concocted . . ." His voice trailed off. He got to his feet, looked pensively out to his glacier.

"The Aleuts told the Russians the mainland was Alyaska or Alaksu, meaning 'Great Land.' And that it is. Everyone knows she's more than twice as large as Texas." He tips his hat, "Sorry about that. But did you know that Alaska is as large as our twenty-one most easterly states put together? In fact, north of Glacier Bay, west of Juneau, we've got a glacier, bright and blue, just like my girl Sapphire," pointing to the face of a big glacier up above us, "that's larger than Rhode Island. In fact, there's a greater concentration of glaciers up here than anywhere in the world, with one-fifth of all the world's fresh water locked up in 'em."

"You know, Padre," he says to me, "I've traveled the tortuous Alaska coast from Ketchikan on up. It's 33,000 miles long, more than the rest of the United States coast combined. And of course, everyone knows it has Mount McKinley, that heaves its peaks above 20,000 feet, higher than any in the whole Western Hemisphere. And something else, Alaska has more grumbling, sizzling volcanoes than any place on earth."

Bill was really cranked up today. I slowed him down with, "Hey, come off it. You heard what the Texan told an Alaska braggard?" He quickly split in, "I'm not braggin'. These are facts—but what did the Texan say?"

"He said, 'If you new arrivals on the scene don't quit blowin' snow, a few of us Texans will get ourselves a few blowtorches, go all around that coast, melting you down so's you'll fit inside Rhode Island'."

Bill puckered his face, "Just like so many who think of Alaska, then see in their mixed up brain nothing but ice and snow. I'd like to see where else you can grow 75-lb. cabbages, carrots as big as your forearm, and beets as big as your head. And where else can you go for three months without turning on your lights?

"In fact," he looks right at me, "I'm gonna prophesy. Some day the whole middle Yukon valley will open up to farmin', so will the Kuskokwim, and large areas out toward Dillingham. All that country has great possibilities. You yourself recall the early days, all the steamers on the way up from St. Michaels to the gold fields. They used to stop at Holy Cross mission on the middle Yukon. Travelers for 20 years marvelled at the farms there with huge lush gardens, pigs, chickens, cows and horses. And that was before all this scientific fertilizer, vernalization of seed, and fancy equipment was known. Sure, the Indians and Eskimos aren't farmers by nature, but if we'd ship in a bunch of those Oriental farmers, we'd see all that country blossom out.

"And I'm gonna prophesy somethin' else. That whole Anchorage area, down the Kenai peninsula, out across Cook Inlet over towards the Valley of Ten Thousand Smokes—for sightseein', recreation, and just plain livin', it's hard to beat. As all these Asiatic wars cease, and as industrialization comes to the Orient, that area'll have cities rivalin' Portland, Tacoma and Seattle. A long time ago, Rezanov, a friend of Baranov, said that 'whoever controls Alaska, controls the Pacific.' Fantastic already, Alaska's trade with Japan. Did you know that about half of Alaska is west of Hawaii, and that some of Alaska's citizens are closer to the capital of Japan than to Juneau?"

Bill stopped, puffed away at his pipe. "I could," he said, "go on and on. For instance the big game. Outside of Africa, it's the best in the world. Up along the Brooks range, if you can imagine it, there migrates a herd of caribou numbering 300,000. The Kodiak bear stands as high as a basketball hoop. Then there are thousands of giant moose, wolf, black, brown and cinnamon bear. It's really incredible. Out west, the Lord instead of asking Abraham to count the sands on the seashore, would have asked him to count the geese, duck and ptarmigan."

With a gentle twinkle Bill says, "I knew I could pan a load of big nuggets, enough to make your eyes bug. Got enough?" "Just one more question, Old Timer." I got my hands going on this one. "How would you put it all together? How would you say Alaska makes you feel. I suppose I'm asking, 'What does all this grandeur do for you?' "

I doubt if old Bill could make his inner wheels turn without his interminable fiddling and puffing on his pipe. "Well," he said, "Alaska's just different. A man can't get around the fact—there's some sort of mystery up here governing the country. What's as spookie as a six-month night, as weird as a totem pole, has mosquitoes the size of airplanes, and bearded fools like me who just can't quite make the break and go on outside where normal people live! A long time ago her fjords, glaciers and pure waters, the young, jagged mountains towering over silent forests, and the earth beneath your feet full of gold set my heart singing. I don't know, but the mystery of the long night, and the challenge of the hard winters, it climbs right into your innards and runs through your blood. Let me try an' explain that.

"With a kind of fierce love, Alaska takes hold of a boy like he was raw ore. It shovels him out and separates him from the common ground. It crushes, sifts, washes and then gently pans away the dirt and tailings. In the end it leaves a real gold nugget. I've watched it happen all these years. I'm glad I'm up here. I'm nourished every day with purity, harmony, beauty and silence. It tells me who I am, what life's about, and where it's goin'. The vast wilderness is the greatest single resource up here."

I walked off wondering. Bill sat serenely puffing and rocking.

ALASKA'S MARINE HIGHWAY

It was a brilliant afternoon in August; we stood at Pier forty-eight in Seattle looking up to the four decks of the steamer Malaspina, as white, clean and graceful as the gulls which playfully carved the sky above us. Often along the cruise we noticed with excitement the seven golden stars of the Big Dipper and the North Star, symoblic of Alaska's flag, painted on the blue, streamlined stack high above the four decks. Before we knew it Seattle was a neatly placed city of scrubbed toy buildings off in a distance. Above and below were the rich blue of sky and water as the mighty twin propellors churned the sea white; we had begun our 1,200 mile trip up the fabled and majestic Inside Passage to Skagway, Alaska, gateway to the Klondike.

Puget Sound, the straits of Juan DeFuca, Gulf Islands, Georgia Strait, Queen Charlotte Sound, Lynn Canal; with stops at Ketchikan, ancient (by west coast reckoning) Wrangell and St. Petersburg, Juneau, and finally Skagway; with towering mountains, breath-taking glaciers, America's greatest fjords—who wouldn't get excited!

That first night out, for a full hour, all on board gazed at the simple mystery of sunset. Tired of lolling about in his vast, private, blue paradise, the sun slipped behind the evening haze as if to dress for cocktails. In a moment the clouds turned into flowing savannahs of burnished orange as fine and delicate as shot silk. Like secluded trysting arbors for passionate lovers, a betwitching array of Gulf Islands steepled with lofty, green pines, stood noble and silent in homage to the utter beauty of the evening sun, just as they had almost two-hundred years previous when Spanish explorers navigated these waters. I could have stayed there forever.

On top deck we watched the stars come out, like someone "up there" pricking holes in an opaque dome allowing heaven's brilliant light to stream down to us. Soon a billion stars were set winking, while the Milky Way divided the sky, stealing glory from Cassiopeia, the Pleiades, Libra and Cancer. It was a shame to close one's eyes to sleep that night. But it was even more so the following night when the Aurora Borealis, decked out in chartreuse and amber, pantomimed in eerie silence across the full stage of the heavens, amongst the footlights of the stars, a spectacular ballet of light. Curving, gyrating, swishing, running fast, disappearing and appearing; only the bright dawn can put to flight these mysterious spirits who abide in the secret caverns of the northern skies.

Each of the three mornings along the serpintine route the sun had to climb steep slopes before gently peeking at us from between sharp peaks. As though a conductor had called a symphony into action, lush, untouched forests greened, and dark sea waters came to life; white gulls followed as if tied by a string, diamond-studded salmon leaped clear of the waters, black, shiny porpoise retreated before our monstrous hull. Gentle breezes caressed us as we gazed and gazed. Only the captain it seemed must know the secret route and channels of the Inside Passage for we were perpetually boxed in by forested mountains and misty islands as serene as isolated hermitages for praying monks. (Only once, and briefly, did we break through into the open waters of the ocean.) Someone said of it all, "as enchanting as Cleopatra's bosom!"

Above Prince Rupert, where the coast becomes Alaska, we encountered tier upon tier of hummock-like mountains rising immediately from the water's edge. Covered with close pines, they appeared as a herd of mammoth, shaggy-humped buffalo reclining on the flat blue plains with even mightier snowcapped mountains corraling them. By the end of the second day we knew the feelings of Russian, Spanish and English explorers who gazed from their three-masted ships at the virginal forests untouched by the saw or axe of man, uncluttered with his debris and pollution. We must have seen ten-thousand hills and mountains that no man has yet climbed. Encircled by this fairy land of harmony and beauty I wondered could anyone living in such surroundings possibly have a problem in the world. Such is the impression it all makes upon the mind and heart.

Leaving Juneau on the morning of our third and last day we entered the famous Lynn Canal. All along the narrow course massive hulks of stone rose sheer from the waters. Capped with jagged spires they were nature's cathedrals, diminishing to pedestrian proportions mere works of man like Notre Dame and St. John Divine. Fierce, naked crags, awaiting the wooly-white snows of winter to clothe them, and decorated here and there with velvet-like moss, stabbed at the sky above. Colossal pyramids of highly mineralized basalt, fashioned, one fancied, by the gods with lightning and thunder as hammer and anvil in the mythical caves beyond this world, heaved upwards. Around them draped the hanging turquoise glaciers, spilling over from the ice-cap that rests along the summit of the immediate coastal mountains for more than one hundred miles.

The first excitement and awe vanish as the eye beholds glacier after glacier off to one side and then the other; rivers of ice, frozen in torrential patterns with mounds, flashing spires, deep crevices; shaping and shaped by the rough shoulders of the abiding, giant mountains, "flowing" down to the blue-white silty sea, carving out fjords, and calving icebergs.

Before we knew it the deep bellowing of the steamer announced Skagway, where overnight in 1898 was born what one goldseeker called, "a town little better than a hell on earth." Soon it would boast twenty-thousand people and Soapy Smith, the most notorious of Alaska's gold-rush bad men. According to customs office records, five thousand people landed in February of 1898 alone. Ahead lay the White Pass, where three thousand horses died along the trail; Bennet Lake where prospectors lifted sails on barge, boat and raft to catch the spring winds to sail seventy miles into the Yukon River onward toward Dawson and the gold fields.

In picture or word no brochure can adequately describe the incredible and continuously spectacular beauty of the Inside Passage to Alaska, but perhaps the same could be said of those other Alaskan scenic wonders: McKinley National Park, encircling that greatest of American peaks, with glaciers forty miles long; Katmai National Monument, across from Kodiak Island, within whose boundaries rest the now quiet craters that gave the name to the Valley of Ten Thousand Smokes; and Glacier Bay National Monument, northwest of Juneau, where summer and winter dwell together among Alaska's greatest glacial spectacle.

Then there is the raw, rugged, unsurveyed Alaska desert beyond the Brooks Range, extending over five hundred miles from east to west, and one hundred and fifty miles northward to the Arctic Sea. With less than four inches of precipitation a year, almost totally uninhabited, the silence is like thunder and the stillness like nothing one has ever experienced. It is America's greatest remaining wilderness.

THE NATIVE PEOPLE TODAY

In this land—larger than Texas, California and Montana together—there has probably never been more native Alaskans than there are today, some 55,000 Indians, Eskimos and Aleuts. Relatively speaking they were left quite alone until the advent of World War II when a great surge of activity ensued to protect North America from Japan and later Russia.

The famous or infamous (depending on whether you enjoyed the drive up or not) Alaska Highway was cut through with astonishing haste from Great Falls, Montana, up through Canada, to Fairbanks. Military installations like Elmendorf and Richardson at Anchorage, Eielson and Wainwright at Fairbanks; communication sites, DEW-line stations all became pipelines for our way of life to pour into every corner of Alaska. Natives were conscripted for military service or enlisted into the all-native Scout Battalions, and today in every sizable village (150 people) a corrugated National Guard Armory stands above their simple huts like spired churches once did in European villages.

While the native peoples are tough—having been able to conquer perhaps the most fierce environment known to man, and having been able to sustain a viable, happy culture through centuries—they are also gentle, and now on the verge of irreparable damage by our aggressive, hard-driving, technological society. By nature the Alaskan peoples are highly tolerant, demonstrating, in the best sense of the word, a passive, live-and-let-live attitude toward life. While this has been their coin of success against the forces of nature—enviable patience, endurance, acceptance—it is also their nemesis when trying to grapple with problems of acculturation.

Today these people cannot live a genuine native life as did their ancestors; that era has vanished. They are, on the whole, unable as yet to fit their lives to the hours of the clock, and the insane competition demanded by our life-style. Pulled by instinct and habit to the past, driven by necessity and survival to grapple with the future, they find themselves in an unenviable, no-man's land between two cultures; and a man without a culture is a man without self-identity, a man without the touch-stones of values, success, development. He is a man suffering.

It is into their cultural vacuum that pour forces worse than the coldest temperatures and more fierce than the wildest bear. Feelings of anxiety, inferiority, insecurity and loneliness grow apace with their newly-imposed expectations of the white-man's ambitions, life-style, possessions.

On the positive side infant mortality has dropped sharply, medical and educational facilities have become available to an increasing degree, resource study and development, as well as relocation programs for families desiring a "new life"—all these are efforts to mend the hurt unconsciously inflicted. The native Alaskan, known for his inventiveness, has chosen from our culture items of special value such as the rifle, motorboat and snowgos—now an integral part of his life.

In urban settlements such as Bethel, Nome, Kotzebue and Barrow (population about 2500) unemployment can reach as high as eighty percent in the winter months. In city areas such as Fairbanks, Anchorage and Juneau we find Alaska's largest settlements of natives (it is said that Seattle has more native Alaskans than does any village within Alaska). The natives, completely out of their familiar environment, have a particularly difficult time. Perhaps the greatest positive note of hope is the growing number of native children who are graduating from high school, with many going on to college. For example, at the University of Alaska at College, just outside of Fairbanks, there are some 250 natives pounding the books alongside whites.

While no one who has anything to do with the Alaska scene can ignore or be content with this inequitable situation imposed on the natives by our arrival in the northland, we can for purposes of this pictorial book put it in focus. Throughout man's history, cultures have confronted one another, exchanged, enriched, harmed and limited one or the other. Within Alaska we see one of the most unique examples of an integrated culture from deep out of the past confronting in a very brief period of time the most highly developed technological culture in the world.

Writing of such problems in such a beautiful pictorial book as this may seem incongruous, but isn't the life and death struggle of the seasons, and the unenviable fight for survival of every species of wild animal something of a paradigm of what man should expect to encounter in his own evolution? If we could only contemplate sufficiently the lessons of nature's beautiful handiwork, and the images of courage from the animal world, perhaps we could come to a deeper harmony, a wiser conspectus, and a more sensitive entrance into the problems of human society.

VILLAGE ALASKA

Nulato, Tanunak, Eek, Selawik. Like strange stars scattered across the map, names like these make up what we might call Village Alaska. About one hundred and seventy-five villages with a median population of one hundred and fifty-five people typify a life-style unique to all America. These villages rest over a lazy bend on the Yukon or Kuskokwim rivers, nestle at a lagoon below a smooth hillock on the Aleutians, lie within the shadow of a towering mountain along the southeast coast, or are just there or here for no apparent reason. Fewer than a dozen of these villages have a connecting road. Outside travel is largely by air. Neighboring, hunting, or fishing is by snowgos or kickers (motorboats). The dogs are about gone.

In the dead of winter when the land itself sleeps, a strange feeling comes upon the outsider who flies over these remote islands of life. Far from television, telephone, stoplights, paved roads, gaudy neon signs, and glittering shopping stores, life-style cannot but be different.

Whether one looks down on Metlakatla, closest village to Seattle; Point Barrow, 1,300 miles north in the cold Arctic; or Nicolai or Atka 2,000 miles west on the foggy Aleutians, the question arises, "Why?" "How?" To dwell there is to have an answer. Friendliness is as present as fresh, unpolluted air; genuine life as patent and inviting as the clear laughter of children. Community emerges at the general store, bingo games, at the biweekly mail plane, the hunter's return, or at the movie. (I recall my first movie at Tanunak on Nelson Island. To outsiders the show-house might be just an oversized shack, but in the village, people, not buildings, are first. Several women carried tin cans for their own snuff spitting, and for the urinating needs of small children. All of us squatted on what we'd call kneelers in a Catholic Church. So incongruous, I thought, viewing a science fiction movie in these environs where man is still largely "the gatherer." But they did pay hard cash to get in.)

An outsider is immediately struck by the quality of life—the leisurely pace, the time given to joshing, and just being together. What wasn't done today, will wait for tomorrow, or the next day. Aggressive efficiency is not the most coveted virtue. Native homes are extremely modest, mostly clean. Small, even cramped inside, little or no paint outside. Families are larger, children quieter. Laughter and smiles seem more common. There is a wide spectrum of tolerance for differences. Seldom does anyone lock-up anything. The few white homes, mostly of teachers and government employees, are large, apart, and painted.

Each village is in some sense a "company town." The Bureau of Indian Affairs, much maligned, sometimes unjustly, controls most of the money, the paid jobs, the future. One church or another plays a dominant role. One village might be 95 percent Episcopalian, another 95 percent Catholic, another 95 percent Orthodox. Sad to say there are often too many denominations fruitlessly competing.

Each village has two distinct existences; one in summer, the other in winter. At breakup time, from early May on the Yukon, to late June on some northern rivers, life sings its richest melodies. The sun like a rich, happy king lolls around most, if not all, of every twenty-four hours. Myriad wild flowers bloom, green grass is everywhere, and the fish begin to move. Everyone gets outside, everyone laughs, and works, and simply feels that life is good.

The chill of autumn gives birth to worries about adequate food, sending the kids off to school, getting things ready for winter. Snow piles high, darkness dominates, paths and riveredge disappear. A stark, cold blanket of ice and snow brings a fixed silence. Is it any wonder that perhaps the most beautiful quality of the native is his own silence, patience and endurance—all bred from the land?

Twenty years ago more than 60 percent of the natives lived in places of fewer than 100 people. Today less than 30 percent do so. Urbanization, a worldwide phenomenon, has not passed by Alaska. For the Indians, Aleuts and Eskimos it means Anchorage, Fairbanks, Juneau, Nome, Bethel, Kotzebue, Barrow, though the last four named have about 2,000 people each. As birth-control becomes more popular, as a greater percentage of villagers go off to high school, and jobs surface in the urban centers, village Alaska may melt like snow and disappear. So many reasons demand that it continue. Here a native, aboriginal people keep alive a unique culture, a fascinating contribution to the variety and wonder of our planet earth. And here, where people know each other extremely well, where life is simple, even austere according to our affluent customs, friendship, that item ever so essential to mans' happiness, breaks through the prism of village life in a more highly nuanced and differentiated fashion, than in our familiar city life where each is so often a stranger, part of the "lonely crowd." Here in this isolation (it is that only to those who do not belong) man is compelled to depend upon and to exercise in a far more radical way his own personal, inner resources. And what else is life all about? I think it is this aspect of authenticity and simplicity which so entices and awakens a resonance in visitors from "the outside."

SOURDOUGH BILL AND TWO SWEETHEARTS

Up the highway from Valdez, off on a trail, one can come to the picturesque cabin of an old prospector, Bill Cooper. We had become great friends. One day with the lofty mountains looking down on us, and the green summer grass covering the hills below, I asked, "Bill, what does a man like yourself do if he's not sluicing or panning gold?"

"You know," he said, touching the brim of his worn hat, "when a man's livin' alone, his mind does some funny, yet delightful things. You'll no doubt laugh when I tell you about my two lady friends." Beneath his shaggy brows, two playful eyes blinked a couple of times. "I make love to one in the summer, the other in winter. One enchants me by day, the other woos me by night. Sapphire here," he pointed over his shoulder with his whittling knife to the deeply creviced glacier that loomed above his sluicing works, "is my summertime gal. She's got the most seductive curves you've ever looked on, and coursin' through her whole being is the bluest of blood. She's so full of mystery, I get goose-bumps thinkin' about her."

When I asked Bill about the blue of glacial ice, he laughed about the way tourists try to chip and procure a piece of the tantalizing blue. "That's why Sapphire's like a woman. You can look at her beauty, admire it, even touch it—but you can't possess it."

Bill scratched his beard, let go with a good load of whiskied snuff, "Like most females, Sapphire's always restless, agitating. See those heaps of rocks piled at her feet? She's a living giant, always movin', shearin' big rocks, and scoopin' out gullies. Nothin'll stop her. All summer she's a workin'. When I lay in my bed, I can hear her, and when I'm at my own diggin's, she's still goin'. It's only when winter comes that there's any rest. She covers herself in soft, white blankets and waits for another spring." Then with a note of sadness, "I've gotten old and wrinkled over the years, but not her. She's still as young, fresh and beautiful as the day we met, and still lookin' forward to a few more decades of showin' off. My, she's a marvelous woman. I'd really miss her if she ever melted and ran off."

It was evident that the old duffer really was attached. I couldn't allow him to get maudlin, so I interrupted with, "And what about your other gal, Bill?"

Immediately a new twinkle came. "I'd sure love to introduce you to the most exotic dancer in the whole north country, but she doesn't come on till winter darkness sets in. She tosses around the greatest assortment of colored gowns you've ever seen—all sorts of gentle reds, greens and pinks." Laughingly he said, "You should see her dance of the seven veils! That's my girl, Aurora."

The Sourdough looks up at me with, "You know, Padre, of all the sights in the northland, I don't think any fifty of 'em together can compare with a first-rate display of the Aurora Borealis. At times from invisible hangers the Aurora drapes across the vast sky, foldin' and unfoldin', even swayin' back and forth. On other nights they squirm up over the horizon like the tail of a gigantic kite, crossin' the heavens, to disappear over some mountain rim. They can blast open right above you, and out of the dark sky rays bend from a central spot to all points of the compass like a netted dome. At times there's somethin' sensuous; all that undulatin' and roamin' about in utter night silence. Legend has it that it's her gyrations that sets the North Wind to howlin' and stirs up the snow storms. That's my girl, Aurora. I watch her dance night after night every winter. She's always lovely, discreet and inventive. She never seems to tire of dancing for me. I never tire of payin' her homage. She's given me her beauty, her grace, and countless hours of delight. Somethin' I couldn't buy with all of Alaska's gold and oil."

URBAN ALASKA

If "urban" is an asset today, then Alaska is holding on to a dirty penny, but if it is a liability, and many contend that it is, then Alaska is really flush. With a total population of about 300,000, and with Anchorage and the surrounding area gobbling up something approaching one-half, there isn't much left over to fashion an urban Alaska with—that is if one insists on using outside standards. But according to the way Alaskans see it, any place with as few as 2,500 would be so classified. Like so much of life it is all relative.

Juneau was the first "large" population center, having come to life when Joe Juneau rolled his pan and saw, beneath the black sand, a heavy line of bright yellow gold dust. That was in 1880. Twenty years later at the turn of the century, taking the honor from Sitka, it was named the capital of the Territory of Alaska. A "little San Francisco" of narrow, winding streets and wooden stairways which climb steeply to homes on the hillside, Juneau today boasts a population of 10,000, with another 4,500 in the general environs and across the narrow Gastineau Channel in Douglas. From the mountainside above Juneau the drab, gawky ruins of the mammoth Alaska-Juneau mine-mill complex stare silently down on the city like sentinels from a past age.

Juneau, ranking third in size, is a modern American city; the economy is supplemented by tourism, fishing and lumbering, a recently erected college, but the city depends most heavily upon its role as capital of Alaska. Much of the gold that Joe Juneau first sighted still lies beneath the heavy mountains—who knows!

Fairbanks goes back to the turn of the century when E. T. Barnette got stuck with his stern wheeler on the Tanana River. He back-paddled and cached his cargo on the Chena River, the present location of the city. He didn't have to worry much about the future for just about that time Felix Pedro let out with a holler of "gold!" The rush was on and so was Fairbanks. Though its population has been like a yoyo, the city boasts 23,000 people, calls itself "The Golden Heart of Alaska", and intends to keep on growing.

Dusty, narrow streets, a sprinkling of log cabins and early day saloons in and around the city remind the visitor of her pioneer past. Although Fairbanks has modern stores, mostly paved streets, plush restaurants and tourist accommodations, it really hasn't given up a wonderful freshness of spirit and attitude. Perhaps its the tough winters that keep alive that early spirit—temperatures can get as low as 65 degrees below zero, and they do. You plug your car in at night like it's a waffle iron wanting heat, and when you drive off in the morning the brief bump-bump reminds you that the bottom of the tire has frozen in its unrounded contour. Lifeblood is pumped into the city, not from gold, though there is some mining in the area; but by the oil industry, tourism, college services (The University of Alaska is located on the outskirts of Fairbanks in the community named "College", and boasts an extremely attractive campus, as well as preeminent departments in solar sciences, anthropology and wildlife). Fairbanks is also a supply depot and a point of focus for all communities west and north.

Anchorage began as a rough construction headquarters for the building of the Alaska Railroad in 1914. It was to run from Nenana (sixty miles southwest of Fairbanks) south to Seward. The railroad was a long time abuilding, and Anchorage inched upward, but even at the outbreak of World War II it was only 4,000. When the Japanese bombed Dutch Harbor on Unalaska Island, and shortly after invaded the islands of Attu, Agattu and Kiska, a stir was caused across America like an anthill being kicked. Immediately the slumbering community of Anchorage, and all Alaska, became militarily significant. To this day the growth, development and concern for Alaska begun then has not stopped. Without this tragic history of war and its aftermath Alaska would never have attained statehood.

With both Fort Richardson and Elmendorf Airbase on the periphery of the city, Anchorage is still influenced in a major but decreasing way by the military, though it is also Alaska's most important port, both by air and sea. The city has an attraction all its own, resting on a flat plain, cradled by the majestic Chugach range, and overlooking serene Cook Inlet. Climate-wise due to the Japanese Current its average yearly mean-temperature rivals Minneapolis, Chicago or New York. January is the coldest month, but even then it often thaws.

Ketchikan, Alaska's most southern urban center, is much like Juneau residing back-to-back with lofty forested mountains. It is traditionally known as the "Canned Salmon Capital" and also as a place for rain, with an incredible average of fourteen feet a year. Houses here as in all the urban cities look just like those in our lower forty-eight, yet there are small colonies of native dwellings in this or that corner. Fishing and lumbering are the life sources here.

Other urban centers, by Alaskan terms, are Valdez and Cordova on the Gulf of Alaska, Sitka and Wrangell along the Inside Passage; Seward, Kenai, Soldotna and Homer on the Kenai Peninsula, and Kodiak, that most ancient of Alaskan settlements, are also in the category of "urban" though they average only about 2,000 people. Just north of Anchorage lies Palmer, hub of the famous Matanuska Valley farming community, with an area population of 6,000. It could pass for a small midwestern farm town. It should be noted that all of these major Alaska communities are south of the Anchorage area. Fairbanks is the only city within the whole vast interior, but on the far western coast we have Bethel—"cultural center for Southwest Alaska"; Nome, with two radio stations and about 150 miles of road; Kotzebue, above the Arctic Circle; and Barrow on the northernmost tip of our continent. They average out to about 2,500, providing "city life" for the surrounding villages. The unique feature of these centers is that they are at least 75 percent native, and a different life-style abides even for the whites simply because accepted urban amenities have not yet arrived.

Population will increase around Anchorage, Fairbanks and Valdez, but perhaps the most upcoming area is the Kenai Peninsula where farming, lumbering, recreation, oil development and a rather pleasant climate all converge. No matter what the coming growth factor is, for decades to come the call of the wild will ever typify the Great Land.

GOLD FEVER

A man was squatting over the edge of the sparkling stream, felt hat tilted against the sun, hands reaching down between his knees. He was panning gold. Downstream, a snoose-spit away, was his sluice box. A large-bore rifle rested against a nearby post. A narrow, crooked path, flanked by tall, waving grass stretched thirty yards to a primitive, hand-hewn log cabin. A huge, shaggy bear skin, claws extended, possessed one side; calcified moose antlers loomed from beneath the front gable. Off to the right on stilts was a cache house where the prospector kept his grub.

I watched the bearded figure dip, agitate, sift and toss, all in one expert motion, over and over. I knew he was a real sourdough (a rare commodity these days even in Alaska) both by his panning and the way he tolerated the confounded mosquitoes.

After dinner, by the light of a kerosene lamp, Jeremiah Flynn sent shivers down my spine and pierced my brain with awe. Shifting and shining like two large nuggets, his hypnotic eyes fixed me in my seat. I knew the fever was on, that he was under the spell of the ghost of gold, that spectre who haunts every stream and mountain in Alaska even to this day.

Jeremiah stared at me, speaking in a strange voice. "I am every man who is driven by the ghost of gold. After the stampede to California in '49, I stood on the streets of Sacramento and San Francisco and felt the pull of all points of the compass. I spit in my left hand, smacked with my right fist, and whichever way it squirted, that's where gold called me. I tramped to Mexico, to Virginia City in Nevada, Last Chance Gulch (Helena) Montana, and up through Oregon and Washington to the Cariboo Trail in British Columbia. It took me a full fifty years to really crack Alaska.

"Before the great rush to Dawson in '98, I had literally blazed trails up a thousand canyons and panned a million streams. Over the years, sweating, swearing, and lusting for gold I climbed up over the Chilkoot Pass from Skagway, prospected down the Tanana, Kuskokwim and Susitna, up the Porcupine and Chandalar. I was seriously abuilding Juneau and Douglas in the seventies; we turned the pages of history at Sitka and made it a gold town by the eighties. I sluiced at Kantishna, rocked and washed at Eagle, laid claims at Ididerod, and sank shafts on the Porcupine.

Like at a seance where one is in contact with the spirit world, Jeremiah didn't move a muscle. His sockets were gaping holes and their two nuggets seemed on fire as he told of the rush of '98. "Dawson began the great finds. Like a great comet of light, the Yukon and Alaska were in the eye of the world. One-hundred-thousand men, and a few women, were struck with the fever, and came as naive as farm boys going to battle. I saw them freeze to death on the winter trail, go insane from the long night, drown in the spring rapids; racing, madly to strike it rich. As quick as a flash in the pan Skagway became a city of 20,000. Depending on whether you were going in or coming out of the Klondike it was either the end or beginning of civilization. In a mere six years the Klondike, like a giant anthill with men furiously moiling below and above, gave $100,000,000 in gold.

"In 1900, having failed at Dawson, I heard of Lindberg panning $10,000 in eight days from the sands of the Bering Sea. He created a stampede to a place later called Nome. In two years it was a town of tents and shacks, of almost 8,000 men and 50 women. Steamers and three-masted whalers lay at anchor in the harbor, and in their very shadows men sluiced and rocked the sands for gold.

"In 1902 I was again driven mercilessly by the spirit. It all began with the big find of Felix Pedro. I threw up buildings on the Chena slough, panned at Skoogey Gulch, sank shafts at Fox and Chataneka, put in stamp mills at Ester. I also raced the 450 miles from Valdez, hoofing with hundreds of others from roadhouse to roadhouse, Eureka, Tonsina, Copper Center, Tazlina, Donnelley's—they're still there today. In just four years Fairbanks had a population of 8,000.

"From all these rough, muddy camps I made Seattle and Portland boom; thousands gathered on the docks to watch the incredible spectacle of millions of dollars in gold brick, nuggets and dust be unloaded. Across the nation and over the world, people read about me in the headlines. I attracted innocent farm boys from Kentucky and Tennessee, prostitutes from Butte and Denver, dancehall girls ($1.00 a waltz) from San Francisco, adventurers from France, England and Australia. I wore diamonds and furs enough to make a New York dandy's eyes dazzle. Nothing, nowhere could equal the delirium and ferment, nor the brotherhood and humor of our hard-living, hard-drinking camps. The fever's hard on a man—it shortens his life, makes him forget home, and builds up a ferocious hunger in him for gold, but it does keep down boredom."

As the sun began peeking at us from the east, the fever had lifted, and Jeremiah had closed his eyes. I sat freed from the grip of his eyes and exhausted from the force and power of his tale. As I climbed out of Gold-Stream Valley I had an awareness I'd never had before. It was a fever that had sent men by the tens of thousands sprawling across Alaska more than eighty years ago, and still grips a man if he allows it.

In 1910 Nome had a population of 14,000, but four years later it had shrunk to a mere 1500. Fairbanks was up to 4000 by 1910, but ten years later it was down to 3000. No one knows how high the white population had climbed (Skagway alone had gone from nothing to 20,000), but by 1915 the tide had ebbed, the rush was over, a part of history, and the white population became a mere 32,000, about the same as the native population. Alaska, however, would never be the same.

THE OIL BOOM

The Muscovite fur rush was a blast, and the Klondike gold rush a fantastic trip, but when measured alongside the present, long-range oil rush, they're like candles against the sun in terms of dollars.

It is conjectured that before the exploratory punchboard activity in the northland is done, Alaska will be recognized as that favored piece of God's good earth possessing the world's greatest known deposits of oil. The economy of the state of Alaska today is made up largely of the salmon and king-crab industries, pulp and forestry products, tourism, and of course government, but all of these will be dwarfed by the literally billions of dollars in royalties attached to oil resources.

Like a brilliant, marvelous comet, the cry "oil discoveries" sped across Alaska, the United States, and even to Europe. For those who were compelled to deal with the problems of economy, development and stockholders it was a great light, but the conservationists, in one great united response shouted, "It is dangerous and could even destroy Alaska's wilderness." They demanded that the oil interests desist until every possible precaution could be taken. And then to really tangle the whole thing, the native Alaskans protested, "The state cannot sell or even lease the land. Our aboriginal rights hold precedence." And so the forces of oil, conservation and native land claims are joined in a spectacular wrestling match. This is an account of the first stones lagged in the game of oil which will influence Alaska forevermore.

First word of the strike came in January, 1968, when it was announced that a well, Prudhoe Bay State No. 1, had flared "a substantial flow of gas" at 8,500 feet. Although the strike was a long time coming, few in the oil industry were surprised. During the 1940's and 1950's testing by the U.S. Navy had indicated quite clearly that there was oil in the arctic. After the first and second wells, in rapid succession new wells totaling thirty came in. Every large oil company in America wanted "in," and on September 10, 1969, at the Sydney Lawrence auditorium in downtown Anchorage, oil men, bankers, state officials and ordinary citizens gathered for the opening of bids on 450,000 acres on the North Slope beyond the Brooks Range. By the day's end Alaska had collected $900 million for its oil and gas concessions in the richest lease sale in history.

In one day Alaska had a bankroll yielding nearly $200,000 per day in interest—talk about a gusher! But add to this the $45 million a year in royalties from already producing wells in Cook Inlet and on the Kenai Peninsula, and one easily grasps the significance of the oil find for Alaska. What a difference it will make—Alaska's annual budget in 1969 was only $154 million, and the state has been dependent upon the military for $4.00 of every $10.00 spent in the state.

The contestants in the fracas all have their points. The oil people rightly contend that Alaska sorely needs the funds to build a viable economy; the natives, comprising 20 percent of the population and quite destitute as a group, could be helped. It would also free America from a critical dependence on foreign oil resources. On the other hand, the conservationists remind us that the wilderness, more important to man than oil, is fastly become scarcer. The oil they say will perhaps last for fifty years, but getting it out will have done irreparable harm to both flora and fauna. Then the native, whose very survival depends upon a stable ecosystem, wants to have his harpoon in this big deal. How can we, the natives ask, be sure that our own livelihood and way of life won't be harmed or perhaps destroyed.

Can we have both the oil and the wilderness? Is it technically possible to remove the oil without undue harm to flora and fauna? If there must be damage, how much is acceptable? Without a doubt each of the contending groups has valuable input. For instance, in determining the world's weather, no single mass plays a more critical role than the arctic ice pack. Beyond the harm done to polar bear and other life by a major oil-spill, what effect would the oil, indisoluable for decades due to frigid temperatures, have upon the melting and freezing activity of the ice pack and hence upon the air currents which influences all our weather? And it is a fact that the arctic flora has taken thousands of years to form into a tundra mat; so sensitive is it that marks made by vehicles during the second world war are as apparent as if made yesterday. Ecologists express great fear over damaging the sensitive ecosystem, and starting the process of uncontrollable erosion of the permafrost.

A great part of the debate centers on the proposed pipeline from Prudhoe Bay (just east of Barrow) some 800 miles to the ice-free port of Valdez. Already the forty-eight inch pipe is ready to go. The oil people have invested more than $2 billion into the oil project and they are not apt to quit. Nor do the environmentalists feel they have made all the yardage they can. Many conservationists couldn't be happier if the oil were to remain forever beneath the frozen tundra.

And the oil will remain underground until the native land-claims problem is settled. As someone said, "What did the natives—the Indians, Eskimos and Aleuts—own? They must have owned something." If each side listens to the other, if the concern is with more than self, then the oil will flow, and all will profit from it, and the environment will remain habitable and intact.

When oil does begin to flow, and hardly anyone doubts that it will, and within the next couple of years, ten thousand new jobs will be created in Alaska; Valdez will service about one tanker each day—30,000 to 120,000 tons—heading for Puget Sound, or California. By 1977 the oil-flow will have doubled, requiring twenty-seven tankers. Fairbanks no doubt will see one or two refineries built in that area. But who knows the number of non-oil connected jobs that will emerge, or the small related industries that will develop? One thing is certain, the black gold will have its influence on Alaska.

"THAR SHE BLOWS"

The year is 1066. Myriad small Norman boats of war invade the English coast. Along another beach, far off on the coast of Alaska, above the Arctic Circle, three umiaks (skin boats) filled with stalky, fur-clad hunters are maneuvered with paddles out beyond the white breakers where gigantic, one-hundred foot blue whales play, spouting and bellowing, unaware of the presence of these Eskimo whalers. In each umiak disciplined men stand poised with highly crafted harpoons. Upon striking the whale an intricately carved, detachable ivory head separates from the staff, and a long coil of sinew rope, attached to a bladder float, plays out.

The year is 1848. A lone vessel, the 275 ton bark *Superior* passes through the Bering Straits, cruises for a season, and returns with a full cargo of oil and baleen (the baleen or "whalebone" brought astonishingly high prices as stay material for the women's corset industry. Whalers often killed whales for this flexible, stiff material alone. The baleen is part of the mouth apparatus of the whale.) American whalers have discovered the lucrative arctic whale grounds, perhaps the most productive the world has ever known. In time there are more than 350 ships a year in these waters. Vessels even winter at rough, makeshift stations above the Arctic Circle in order to be the first at break-up time. For fifty years this whaling activity brought the white man and his ways, to one extent or another, to practically every native settlement along Alaska's 33,000 mile coast.

San Francisco, Astoria and Seattle all got into the act, though New Bedford, Maine, retained its title as number one whaling port. Particularly at the California port three-masters with sails closely bound, waved like a forest of windblown trees. Rough sailors bartered their own scrimshaw and native-carvings while spinning yarns of that nation of fur and ice far to the north. Rendering plants billowed smoke like the once playful whales spouted water. San Francisco became the second greatest American whaling port, and Alaska was becoming known from coast to coast. Though it seemed easy money, this whaling business was always plagued with tragedy, and the two greatest in all whaling history took place off the coast of Alaska.

The year is 1865; the Civil War is raging. Each side is taking whatever means possible to destroy the other. And so we find the confederate warship, the *Shenandoah,* roving the Pacific plundering every trader, or whaler flying the Union flag. In June of that year she sailed into the Bering Sea, rollicking from one devastating success to another. In one week alone she had set ablaze twenty-five whalers. Up and down the arctic coast for hundreds of miles the story was telegraphed in billows of black smoke from the whale oil and blubber. When captured some protested, "The war is over!" Captain Waddell of the *Shenandoah* refused to believe it and another ship would go up in smoke, until on the second of August, he met a British schooner and learned that indeed the war had been over, that Lee had surrendered at Appomattox almost four months previously. By then the *Shenandoah* had burned or scuttled a total of forty-six whalers. But the fates had yet another major evil calamity in store for the whaling industry.

On November 8, 1871, the New Bedford *Shipping List* carried extra-large headlines: TERRIBLE DISASTER TO THE ARCTIC FLEET. Off Point Belcher above the Circle, the sinister arctic ice pack had changed direction under the fierce, driving force of the North Wind. First the *Oriole,* then the *Monticello* and the *Roman* got trapped by the ice, and soon thirty-three vessels were pinned helplessly by the devilish pack. The grinding and crushing, louder than thunder, foretold doom. In all, twenty-five whalers were crushed and sunk. However the twelve-hundred men, women and children aboard were all saved. Skirting the pack in small whaling boats they rowed sixty miles to the safety of eight vessels which had out-maneuvered the pack. After wintering in Hawaii all made their way back to the east coast where a welcome, proper for those who seemingly had come back from the dead, awaited them.

Just five years later another twelve vessels were crushed by the pack and lost, and the following year another six. Often whole crews were forced to survive inhospitable winters among the Eskimo people.

Such catastrophes piled one upon another by the diabolical ice were more than the whaling industry could absorb. Each year the number of whalers going into the arctic waters decreased. Gradually whaling became part of our history, and so it is today except for three ships, America's total fleet, operating appropriately out of San Francisco. And a good thing that it has become history. Far too long, in far too many villages had the sailors peddled their rum, abused and insulted the people; and far too long had the American government allowed whalers to decimate the herds of the world's largest mammal. Today it is doubtful that the gigantic bowhead and blue whales will survive the plunder and pollution of that tiny mammal, man.

THE CHALLENGE OF CONSERVATION

Take a map of continental United States, count off the twenty-one most easterly states. Alaska is that large, but with fewer people than Miami, Florida. It is actually an incredibly virginal and marvelous park. In these times of ugly, repulsive pol ution in our waters, air and land, what an opportunity for a massive national effort to preserve and perpetuate the beauty and grandeur you so readily appreciate between the covers of this pictorial book. "What can this spring tell us that other springs have not? And yet how willingly and happily we await." But spring can whisper to the human spirit only so long as there is a clean slate upon which to write its message.

If there is to be a happy harmony between necessary development of mineral, water, recreational, and forest resources on one side, and the conservation of pure water, scenic vistas and wildlife on the other, then the state and nation must elaborate a conservation ethic. What is, for instance, more important to Alaska, cattle or the brown kodiak bear, the largest bear on earth? There is understandable confrontation among various groups: commercial reindeer herds conflict with caribou grazing and waterfowl nesting; salmon with logging; and moose with oil exploration. If we carelessly allow development and exploitation of the land, what will happen for instance, to that excellent and extremely important nesting area for the trumpeter swan along the Copper River Delta area? To meet the challenge and to avoid the gross wastage typical of so many other places in our great republic, Alaska more than anything else needs better knowledge of its fauna, flora and resources, and a more sophisticated collation of facts and planning.

A conservation ethic demands that we reshuffle our values, reinterpret our priorities as to what counts in building a planet fit for man. The great fur rush of the Russians depleted the seas of otter until they were almost extinct; seal, walrus, and now the whale, all are threatened with the mark of extinction. The gold rush brought not only the lonely miner with pan and sluice, but the monstrous dredge that built its own floating harbor on the tiniest of streams and then systematically gutted valleys from end to end, draining off all soil, leaving behind nothing but barren, ugly heaps of gravel. It is well that the forces of conservation rally today, as they are across the nation, to protect man's greatest heritage, his natural environment.

An adequate conservation ethic must establish as a final goal not simply the preservation of nature, but to enhance, enrich and maximize life and happiness for human beings. To kill fur-bearing animals is good, to lift minerals from the earth is good, and to pipe oil is good. But if we are to proceed rationally in our pursuit of life, then, it seems to me, we must redefine civilization, restudy the concept of progress, and above all re-educate man's esthetic sense, making sure that beauty is included among the balls he jugg es in his search for happiness.

One cannot but smile at the naiveté and selfishness of proponents of Zero Population Growth, and of those who persist in keeping "Alaska for the Alaskans" (so often these are rather recent whites who fail to realize that they themselves are intruders into native lands). The fact that Alaska is as large as that area of eastern American containing a population of 130 million, where there are still scenic park areas and havens for nature lovers, should say something. In other words one can get overexcited about the ecology thing. For example, the most densely populated nation of the world is not China, nor India, but Holland. And it seems for all that we behold of the Dutch, they are not less happy, nor twitching from claustrophobia, any more than others of the human race.

Certainly in developing a conservation-development ethic we could do worse than to examine the instinctive wisdom of the native peoples in Alaska. For us the environment is something we exploit, for them it is part of existence, like an arm. To offend nature is to offend self, to tear something important in the web of life. Their taboos have been grossly misunderstood by the white man as superstition, when in actuality they were part of an integrated system which kept alive man's awareness of his intimate relationships with his environment and all other life. For instance, when an Eskimo killed a seal, he returned a bit of the intestines or blood to the water, he spoke to the great seal spirit reminding him that he needed to kill the seal, that his own life depended upon it, that they were in this thing together. He then begged the spirit to allow the seal to return again next year.

The native took from the environment only what he needed to live. Exploitation and profiteering were foreign to his mentality. An adequate conservation ethic will ultimately fail unless western, technological man returns to a more integrated concept of life and a greater awareness of those supportive qualities within the environment. He must come to see that a clean air system is as much a part of himself as his circulating blood. The pollution of either is damaging. Like the native we must see that the human person is not an isolated atom, but part of the fabric of life, part of the total environment, with incredible mutual dependencies. Until that happens nature will continue to be seen in terms of resources to be exploited, alien forces to be tamed and dominated.

All too often, because of false intellectualizing within both the secular and sacred spheres, we have looked down on the primitive peoples. They were less "civilized," but in all propriety we must today accept the fact that perhaps it is only these people who can lead us through a polluted environmental crisis to safety. So many values they have that we do not, particularly a sensitivity to life in all forms. Life quality, they tell us, is not dependent upon gadgets, body pampering and conspicuous consumption, but simplicity, friendship and harmony within one's self and with one's environment. In the elaboration of a sound conservation ethic we could do a lot worse than to study respectfully the ways of the indigenous peoples of our land.

THE DISCOVERY OF ALASKA

It was precious June on the inhospitable eastern seaboard of Arctic Russia. The whole tiny settlement of Petropavlovsk (town of Peter and Paul) must have turned out that morning when the Dane, Vitus Bering, and the Russian Alexie Chirikof, of the Tsar's navy, boarded their two ships, the *St. Peter* and the *St. Paul,* on a voyage of discovery out into the Pacific Ocean to the east. And, though we do not know it, the sky must have been bright and sunny as they weighed anchor, unfurled the canvas to catch the pure, spring breezes, to sail forth into the silent east. As the ships disappeared over the horizon those standing on shore listened to the lapping waves and wondered.

Bering had been in the service of the Russian Navy since 1703, as weather beaten as the prow of his vessel, and as wise to the sea as the soaring gulls. He made the first recorded voyage from the Pacific, through what we now call Bering Strait, into the Arctic Ocean, named the St. Lawrence and the two Diomede Islands, and established the fact that Asia was separated from America. (Of course, the Eskimos could have told him this fact!)

We do not know what the Muscovite lookout shouted, but it must have been as exciting and transforming as our own "land, ahoy; land, ahoy!" Though separated by fog after a couple weeks at sea, both ships "discovered" Alaska, the Great Land, on successive days. Chirikof sighted land near Cape Addington on the west side of Prince of Wales Island on July 15, 1741. The next day, the feast of St. Elias, Bering's lookout caught sight of a majestic, snowcapped peak off in a distance, and according to Russian tradition it was named for the saint of the day, Mount St. Elias.

Chirikof sent his mate, Abraham Dimentief, ashore with ten men armed with muskets to reconnoiter. The men did not return. Next day the same thing happened to a second small band of men. With sadness and regret Chirikof, after waiting several precious days, set sail for home, charting the coast and naming islands as he went. Bering and his crew also having touched land, more than 2,500 miles from Petropavlovsk, set sail for the west, but bad weather, diminishing supplies and scurvy began to haunt the *St. Peter.* By the time they reached the far end of the Aleutians the gods above had turned all the forces of nature against that tiny wooden island of men. Howling winds were their war cry, snow and sleet their weapons. Slick ice coated the decks, built upon every plank, and incapacitated the rigging. Scurvy began to count the men; a long dying began on an island of the Commander chain (now called Bering Island) where they dropped anchor to winter.

On board with Bering was an exceptionally capable botanist, George Steller, who until then was frustrated and gloomy. For him, being marooned was ecstatic. Delighted with the rare opportunities provided by their island bivouac, he skillfully illustrated by drawing and descriptions the beauty, variety and wonder of both flora and fauna. In fact, without his scientific diagrams and descriptions we would know scarcely anything today of that now extinct mammal, the rhytina or sea cow. (Steller's journal was unknown until 1939 when it was uncovered in the archives of Leningrad.) In one place he describes the abundance of fox: "Today we killed sixty fox. They are so friendly, practically taking food from our hands, that we can scarcely eat in peace."

All during the winter the men labored to survive, but they also piled high furs from the seal, walrus, fox and sea otter, hoping at least for a return of a few rubles. When the remnant sailed into Petropavlovsk a year late, though there was mourning over the death of Bering and twenty others of the crew, the survivors were ecstatic with joy. They had made it, and the furs were easily worth $30,000. Little did that weary crew suspect that those dreadful months of exile were to sound a bugle blast announcing the most astonishing and lucrative fur rush the world would ever know. The pelt of the "bobri morski," or sea otter, soft, fine, lustrous, would entice, excite and drive the Russian fur hunters, the Promishleniki, eastward for more than one hundred years.

As voraciously as an awakened spring bear hungers for food, so the Russians clutched for furs to barter for silk, cotton, tea, spices and, much more, in trade with China. For instance, in 1757 a ship owned by one Trapeznikof, on its way to Canton had as cargo 4,573 sea otter, 1,493 silver fox, 2,115 cross fox, and 1,270 red fox. At prices equivalent to our own time, this cargo would be worth probably $2,000,000.

Diaries record stories of landing on this or that of the many hundreds of small Aleutians; thousands of birds would rise, animals would appear as if by magic. Near the shore herds of seal and otter played; soon blood-red waters lapped at the shores where naked carcasses rotted.

This chase blinded men to their own humanity, made them forget family, home, and even personal suffering. Year after year countless ships sailed out of Russia, hopping in a great arc a distance of more than 7,000 miles along the Aleutians to Kodiak, Prince William Sound, down across the Alexander Archipelago, south beyond the Queen Charlotte Islands to the mouth of the Columbia River, and to California itself. This is the first major factor in the modern development of Alaska. Until then the Asiatic Eskimo, Aleut and Indian people had been alone, untroubled, in the "Great Land" for thousands of years.

ALEKSANDR ANDREEVICH BARANOV

In his work, "Astoria," Washington Irving says of Baranov, "a rough, rugged hard drinking old Russian; somewhat of a soldier, somewhat of a trader; above all a boon companion of the old roystering school, with a strong cross of the bear . . ." An unknown captain reported, "He is continually giving entertainment by way of a parade, and if you do not drink raw rum and boiling punch as strong as sulphur, he will insult you." But this was near the end, after long years of sleeping in wet forests, holding the tiller against raging storms, and felling trees for the building of forts, homes, ships and docks.

Aleksandr Andreevich Baranov more than any single man is responsible for the Russian presence from the tip of the Aleutians to Kodiak, to Sitka, and even to Fort Russ (Ross) in California. In 1792, seven years before our colonies broke with England, Baranov, at the age of 45, landed at Kodiak. For the next twenty-five years even the angels gazed in astonishment at his incredible accomplishments. Picture if you can, over 1,000 Aleut men (conscripted from God knows how many villages), dressed in sealskin and gut clothing, with wooden conical hats, paddling 500 double-holed skin bidarkas (canoes), down the Southeastern coast for hundreds of miles gathering the valuable otter pelts by the thousands. Year after year the enslaved natives plied the coast, dying by war, water and wanton negligence. But let us hear from Baranov himself.

On one occasion weary and worn by the inhospitable climate, the rough, inadequate food, and tired from battling with perturbed segments of his community—disheartened monks, dull-eyed serfs, exiled criminals, anxious natives—he wrote home to Gregory Sheiloff, manager of this Hudson-Bay type commercial company, ". . . you consider me not a friend but a menial . . . not really worthy to manage this colony." Recounting the hardships he confronts his superior; "To me you show limitless greed and cupidity. How you insult me by believing I would break the holy laws of hospitality toward the helpless as you suggest."

Though commanded to retrieve the greatest possible quantity of furs, he saw limitations to what should be done. "Sea otter are not caught like cheap salmon. Our field extends 1,300 miles. The passage to Yakutat (an agricultural colony was attempted here with unwilling Russian serfs in 1797) is hard on the Aleuts. Imagine the poor devils making the journey both ways, 1,300 miles in narrow bidarkas, without sails and only by paddle. They cannot take many supplies, so must endure hunger. They often perish from storms, in constant danger from their blood-thirsty enmies (Tlingit tribes). They do it, but only by dint of constant vigilance on the part of the Russian hunters."

It was this unusual mixture of ruthless commitment to duty, an innate respect for hospitality, and concern for fairness that fashioned Aleksandr Baranov into the Lord of Alaska. He refused to allow Russian-bound employees to take children from the colony, forbade any type of prostitution, encouraged interracial marriage, and consistently fought venereal disease. Every difficult situation he confronted head-on, and never asked his men to go where he wouldn't, nor do anything he wouldn't. To allow expected and unexpected pressures to diminish he always kept a vat of crab apples, rye meal and cranberries fermenting with Kvas yeast. No one else was permitted to distill, but one and all, when off duty, could drink as much as desired.

Within ten years the sea-otter saga had carried the Russian hunters more than 1,200 miles farther east and south from Kodiak. At strategic and advantageous locations they drove off the Indians and built forts. At one place, "on a grassy, level place, at the foot of towering peaks, and looking over an islanded lagoon," they repeated their accustomed pattern of take-over but without reckoning with the strength and fierce pride of the people. They knew the place by the name, New Archangel; we by Sitka. The date was 1799. When the fort was built it was, without a doubt, the finest structure on the whole west coast.

The abused, swindled and humiliated Kolosh, as the Russians called all Indians along southeast Alaska, bided their time. One bright, happy Russian holiday when vigilance at the fort was relaxed, painted Tlingit Indians slipped from the forest to the fort. At sunset the waters were red with the blood of scores of Russian and Aleut men; from the burned fort white smoke, like incense to their gods of war, curled upward. It is the bloodiest and most successful revenge of the native peoples against the Russians ever carried out in Alaska, though a similar incident did occur at Nulato on the middle Yukon forty years later.

Poor Baranov! Constant hardship and near total collapse of the whole commercial and political enterprise seemed like an arrow lodged in his heart. Some recognition of his work did come in 1804. At the age of fifty-seven, this simple tradesman, and adventurer, was made a Collegiate Counselor by Tsar Alexander "for faithful service in hardship and want, and for unremitting loyalty," equal in rank to an abbot or a colonel in the army, entitled to be called "Excellency," and that he was. While this was significant for Baranov, it had wider import —the Tsar was becoming interested in Russia's presence in America.

By 1804 Sitka had been retaken. Here was established the seat of government, the kremlin, for the Russian-American empire in the making. Baranov built a castle atop a prominence on the water's edge. To this place of elegance and joyful hospitality came the greatest sea captains of the day to gaze upon the Lord of Alaska, and view the elegant arts and crafts and general living of his little Russia. Literally around the world—London, Boston, Paris, Canton, and Honolulu—Baranov and his castle-living became legend. With conflicting reports of Baranov reaching Russia, Nikolai Rezanov of the Tsar's court and chief stockholder of the Russian-American Company visited Sitka. He wrote to the Tsar, "We all live poorly at New Archangel, but worst of all lives the founder of the colony. I tell you, gentlemen, he is truly an extraordinary man. His name is famed the length of the Pacific. Bostonians esteem and respect him, savage tribes dread him. While he is overwhelmed with praise by foreign nations, he has to drink the bitter cup of disillusionment at home."

In 1817, Baranov, tired and very old at seventy, set out for the Fatherland, but never reached it. He died at sea, by happy coincidence, in the tropics. This man who had labored for so long in the chilly climates found rest in the warm waters off Sumatra. He had left behind twenty-four settlements or colonies, and a company worth seven million gold rubles. Sitka was a prosperous and civilized center of Russian culture. Oregon and California had nothing to compare.

From our vantage point we may say in a basic sense that the whole adventure was evil. He loved men, and worshiped his God, but he was part of a gross, cultural misconception about nationhood, colonization and the recognition of other peoples. It was a misconception which approved of practically any means to enrich the Fatherland—in this case it allowed the mass, irrational slaughter of fur-bearing animals, and any natives who got in the way.

Perhaps we are kindest when we conclude that Baranov was a product of his own culture and times. In this narrow column of light he lived honorably. Whatever judgment one makes of Baranov it shall always be true that this one man more than any other is responsible for that more than brief moment in history when North America, down even to California, was touched by, explored by and, in one degree or another, claimed by Russia as her own.

BARANOV'S ANNA

St. Paul on Kodiak Island was by 1798 a neat Russian colonial village, not unlike those on our eastern seaboard. A ruddy Kenaitze woman, water pails in hand, followed the path to the beach. Her tight-fitting, long Russian dress showed her firm breasts. She walked straight and proud, and well she should have. Anna, daughter of a Kenaitze chief, had become the wife of Aleksandr Andreevich Baranov. She not only gave birth to his children, Antipatr Aleskandrivich and Irnia Aleksandrovna, she also kept alive the gentler virtues in the breast of the task-driven bear and lord of the Russian-American Company.

Anna was given to Baranov by way of barter, friendship and alliance in 1794. Though she perhaps never realized it, it was the children begotten with her more than anything else that kept Baranov from returning to the Fatherland. And without his bulldog tenacity, the Russian empire along the coast may never have materialized. It was Anna and her people, when all others had deserted Baranov, who continued, no doubt because of Anna, to supply a starving colony. Yearly her father supplied scores of men and bidarkas (canoes) to hunt otter and fight wars. Out of loyalty and fear her tribe watched the young men go off to search for furs, possibly never to return. Indeed, "God is in his heaven and the Tsar is far away!"

Around this woman, Anna, we see the churning and complex forces of grandeur, romance, pathos and tragedy which typify the era. According to any Russian she was a phenomenal success: a nobody taken to wife by a great leader, bearing his children, and ultimately being dubbed by the Tsar himself as a Princess of the Kenai (as though he really owned the area), and had the privilege to send her children to the finest of Russian schools. Yet, the dominant Aleuts resented her, and to the priests she was a symbol of evil, living sinfully with a man who had a true, sacramental wife in Russia. (For all the vibrant life and gentle wisdom in her, Anna could not comprehend the odd and persistent annoyance of the priests. "Why," she wondered, "do they make such a fuss over that one rather unimportant thing? Anyway, someone should sleep with and comfort her Lord.")

In the end she saw her two children sail off to the grandeur of Russia, and almost immediate death from city life. And Baranov, it seems, after settling permanently in Sitka, ten years after their marriage, saw little of her.

An item of barter and alliance, living among strangers, rejected by the dominant church, separated from her children, and apparently deserted by her husband, a gentle, simple woman caught in the vortex of the white man's lust for wealth. This is Anna, a symbol of the destruction brought to the native peoples who happened to live near the fresh, blue waters where the prized otter played.

TEN MONKS

It was late autumn in the year 1794. The whole colony of St. Paul on Kodiak Island was elated—the first ship in more than a year glided into the harbor under full sail. Baranov was oblivious of the joy and excitement. He stood scratching his head, puzzled. On board he distinctly saw bearded men wearing tall, conical hats with long, black robes. Sure enough, down the gangplank from the *Three Saints* came ten austere monks, destined to bring more trouble to the capricious Russian Bear than he ever could have imagined. Was this the answer to his request of four years previous, "Send a clergyman of learning, mild, not superstitious, and not a bigot." Only much later did Baranov discover that these poor monks had been hoodwinked by false representation on the part of Shelikoff, the founder and head of the Russian-American Company. It was on his part all for public-relations and political favors. To have the Orthodox Church established in this far-off land would enhance its attractiveness and the company's considerably.

For personal and policy reasons the monks were soon in open conflict with Baranov. The monks particularly resented having to live in the common bunkhouse with one hundred and fifty hardworking, hard drinking, unwashed men who sweated, snored and smelled in no ordinary degree, and to keep buried memories of home they sang loud, danced hard, and lustily enjoyed the native maidens. Indeed, the poor monks had a case: how, for heaven's sake, could they recite their holy prayers amidst all this! The monks had been told that church and monastery would be finished when they arrived.

Monk Joseph wrote to the powers that be in Russia, "With regard to my work, the Russians are a hindrance because of their depravity (many were criminal exiles) which I find in startling contrast to the strong moral fiber of the untutored natives. I fail to find one good thing about the administration of Baranov. Starvation has stalked this place since our arrival. When we are able, we help ourselves to the open table—digging clams on the beach."

The monks did set up a church, they did enhance the settlement, bringing comfort to the Russians so far off from their own native culture, and they did work constructively with the local tribes.

Four years after their arrival, due to a total ignorance of anthropology (as yet an unknown science), Father Juvenal was murdered near Lake Iliamna, Alaska's largest inland lake—just north of Katmai National Monument. His diary survived and narrates one of the most unusual tales in the lore of Alaska. Juvenal, having made some progress with the people by his genuine concern for them, lost out by his persistent concern for monogamy, seriously insulting and infringing on the prerogatives of the chief. The people turned against him.

"Last night I returned at the usual hour to my cell for prayers . . . in the middle of the night I awoke to find myself in the arms of a woman whose fiery embraces excited me to such an extent that I fell victim to lust." But Juvenal, if nothing else, was most authentic. For this rather innocent "fall" he repents with incredible severity, "I have vowed to burn no more fuel in my cell all winter—a mild punishment when compared to the blackness of my sin." But the poor man would not have to endure the less attractive bedfellow, old man winter. Within days Juvenal underwent a cruel mutilation and death.

Father Nektar, loyal to the letter of the laws of his church, almost drove the native wife of Baranov insane with his incredible arrogance and persistent condemnation of their cohabitation (Baranov had a wife in Russia). And when the colony was rife with problems, it was Nektar who fearlessly became the revolutionary leader of weary, disillusioned Russians and indentured natives. Together they plotted the overthrow of Baranov. The monks were lucky; when the coup failed they received mere imprisonment. Others were hanged by their thumbs and beaten.

Monk Herman, the most outstanding of all, was as correct as a Jeremiah in condemning the outrageous yearly conscription of native men for war and fur hunting. Summer after summer the village women watched their men leave, many never to return. Whole villages drained of male strength and vitality languished and then disappeared. In this regard Herman was truly a voice of conscience crying in a wilderness. But in other areas Monk Herman was successful. In 1969 on Kodiak Island dignitaries of the Russian Orthodox Church, along with guests from other churches, gathered for the canonization of Monk Herman. From then on within the Russian Church he would be known as St. Herman, man of great courage and dedication, proponent to a heroic degree of human and divine values.

Today the greatest living remnant of the Russian period is what these monks brought. Even now some twenty onion-domed Russian churches dot Pacific Alaska; and the Russian heritage is alive in the Orthodox faith of both natives and whites. These men and their followers were responsible for the first schools (there were once five in Sitka), and orphanages in Alaska. They promoted agriculture, irrigation, building trades, taught hygiene and even developed smallpox vaccination (by passing an infected thread through the flesh of a healthy man).

Perhaps the most heralded of the Russian priests was Ivan Veniaminof. He came to Sitka in 1834, learned the native dialects, promoted development, encouraged research and studies, and won people wherever he went. After twenty-five years in Alaska, the man was made Patriarch of Moscow—no mean job, and no mean accomplishment for one so far from the center of things.

AMERICA RAISES HER FLAG

The young and beautiful Princess Maksoutoff, wife of the last chief manager of the Russian American Company, went to bed restless and dejected on the evening of October 17, 1867. She and her husband, Alexi, had been observing the three American ships in the harbor of New Archangel (Sitka) and had been talking of the morrow and their own plans for returning to the Fatherland.

That night the princess had a dream. Dark clouds rolled in from the direction of Russia. All at once she saw the grey ghosts of the hundreds of Russians who had died during the past eighty years of occupancy. With Baranov in the foreground, greyer than the rest, all stood at attention. Invisible hands began lowering the Russian ensign. As if from nowhere several thousand Tlingit and Aleut ghosts appeared in warpaint, with buttocks turned to the descending flag. Thunder cracked, giant bolts of lightning split open the earth, mountains shook, every totem in the land toppled into the sea.

Of course the actual event was not like her dream at all—but then maybe it was. The official government report of the United States Government simply states, "The command of General Davis, about two hundred and fifty strong, in full uniform, armed and handsomely equipped, were landed about 3:00 P.M. and marched to the top of an eminence on which stands the Governor's house where the transfer was made." One flag was lowered, another raised, accompanied by twin salutes from all possible guns and artillery. The cannon echoes, dying far up every canyon and out across the bay, sent an eerie chill up the spine of every Russian. As Governor Alexi Maksoutoff and his Russian compatriots set sail for the Fatherland they knew that on that misty afternoon a gigantic empire, theirs, slid into the sea forever.

The *New York World* bellowed, "Russia has sold us a sucked orange." But that sucked orange of Alaska had within it a power that just wouldn't quit manufacturing juice. Alaska at the price of $7,200,000, cost the United States about two cents an acre. What with the gold rush, the oil rush, the fisheries, forests, etc., we can only smile at the sage advice of the *New York Daily News* of July 16, 1868. "We wish Russia would consent to receive back the territory as a free gift from this Republic. We should deem it a very fortunate riddance." Another commentator felt the people would be against the purchase because it would upset the symmetry of our geographic boundaries!

From purchase to territorial status in 1912, and finally to full statehood in 1958 was a long trip by dog sled. How entertaining it would be to visit the world beyond to overhear present day exchanges between those two friendly connivers and empire dealers, William Seward, Secretary of State, and Edward de Stoeckle, the Tzar's envoy and minister.

"Seward's Ice Box," "Walrussia," "A sucked orange," indeed!

Right: Oceangoing tug maneuvers cargo barges through hazardous ice near Point Barrow on the Arctic Ocean.

Below: Evening sun highlights ball-shaped Arctic cotton atop their vertical stems on the Seward Peninsula. These grasslike plants are often found in damp meadows throughout most of the northern tundra. *Right:* Rugged peaks of the awesome Brooks Range above the Arctic Circle. This mighty range of mountains running east to west spans an area over five hundred miles in length.

Below and Right: Herdsmen standing amidst reindeer prior to ear-marking and dehorning on the Seward Peninsula. The antlers were harvested for export to the Orient. In 1892 with the help of Lapp herdsmen reindeer breeding was introduced in this region to supplement diminishing stocks of whales, walruses and seals.

Below: Eskimos on their way to a council meeting in Tununak on the western edge of Nelson Island. *Right:* Symbols of Christianity mark this cemetery near Tununak. In the background, boats are removed from the water to avoid possible damage from the winter ice.

Below: Hand-hewn blockhouse in Sitka, erected near turn of the 18th century to protect community from the Tlingit Indians. *Right:* You come face to face with the Indian totems preserved in Saxman Park near Ketchikan.

Below: View from the surface of Gastineau Channel details the city of Juneau perched on a narrow shelf. In background, low hanging clouds obscure the massive mountains surrounding this famous capital city. *Right:* Stairway depicts the steep hillside location of Juneau.

Below: Huge chunk of glacial ice creates a grotesque shape on surface of Mendenhall Lake. In background, icy tip of Mendenhall Glacier curves around a waterfall spilling into the lake. Glacier's source is the Juneau Icefield at approximately 4000 feet elevation. *Right:* Looking south from Revillagigedo Island a fishing boat enters the sheltered water of Tongass Narrows near Ketchikan.

Below: Tlingit Indian war canoe on display at Centennial Building in Sitka. *Right:* Sheer face of Mt. Case rises from surface of Glacier Bay to an elevation of 5550 feet in Glacier Bay National Monument. Established in 1925.

Below: Idle gold mine seems determined to win the fight for survival in Hatcher Pass north of Palmer. Diggings from this mine were valued at approximately $20,000,000. *Right:* Brilliant red rose growing wild along the Chickaloon River west of Hope. Wild roses are seen across many areas of the state below the Arctic slope.

Below: A young couple and their dog anticipate limit catch of salmon in the Copper River below Chitina. *Right:* Cattle grazing leisurely near the tidelands of Kodiak Island. This is major beef producing area in Alaska.

Below: Looking south from Portage Glacier late afternoon sun intensifies snow covered peak in Chugach National Forest on Kenai Peninsula. *Right:* A midwinter landscape on the Seward Highway west of Girdwood.

Below: Explorer Glacier inching its way down the slopes of the Chugach Mountains above Portage Creek near the Seward Highway. Rivers of ice flow very slowly—usually only an inch or two a day. A movement of a foot or two a day is considered fast. *Right:* Ever-alert sea gulls survey their domain from cone-shaped rock in Kachemak Bay near Homer. In the background, the Kenai Mountains.

Below: The residents of Tununak are well adapted to ice and snow of midwinter on shore of Bering Sea. *Right:* River tugboats fully packed in ice and snow await the coming of Spring on their ways in Kotzebue.

Below: Storm clouds appear ominous above sunlit gillnet fishing boat below mouth of the Kvichak River on Bristol Bay. This Bay is source of the largest red salmon runs in the world. *Right:* Salmon smoking in a summer fish camp at Klukshu on the Haines cutoff in the Yukon.

Below: Once faithful sternwheelers at rest on the banks of the Yukon River in Whitehorse, Yukon Territory. This capital city was transportation hub during Klondike gold rush. *Right:* The great bend of the Yukon River below its confluence with the Porcupine River near the Arctic Circle. This great river traveling in a semicircular arc from its headwaters in the Yukon Territory covers a distance of nearly 2300 miles. It is equal to distance between New York City and Albuquerque, New Mexico.

Below: Residents arrive in their snowmobiles to meet the mail plane at Tununak air strip on Nelson Island. This flight arrives two days a week, weather permitting. *Right:* Mid-winter in residential area of Kotzebue. This rapidly-growing Eskimo settlement discovered in 1816 lies approximately 30 miles north of the Arctic Circle.

Below: Weathered cottonwood root system lodged against shore of Ingram Creek west of Portage. *Right:* Low-hanging clouds partially envelop Mt. Iliamna, in the Aleutian Range. View looking west across broad expanse of Cook Inlet from Ninilchik on Sterling Highway.

Below: Mower at work in the fertile Matanuska Valley northeast of Anchorage. In background, the foothills of the Talkeetna Range. Due to the long hours of daylight during the summer season, growth of agricultural products is fantastic. *Right:* An Eskimo trapper adjusts his snowmobile on the frozen surface of the Bering Sea.

Below: Surf fishing is a popular pastime in the gentle rolling surf along the eastern shore of Kodiak Island. *Right:* Low growing willow trees partially enveloped with ice, snow near Susitna River south of Mt. McKinley.

Below: Dense forest of spruce trees along the shore of picturesque Tustumena Lake on the Kenai Peninsula. *Right:* Young moose should win struggle with current in the fast moving Russian River near Cooper Landing.

Below: Midday sun shimmers on the surface of Christochina River. On the horizon the crest of Mt. Stanford (elevation 16,208 feet) marks the northwest edge of the Wrangell Mountains. Eight peaks soaring above 12,000 feet dominate this mighty range running west from the Yukon border for a distance of about 150 miles. *Right:* Looking north across a broad expanse of the Copper River and gravel terraces near the ghost town of Chitina. In the distance are the Wrangell Mountains.

Below: Looking East, across the Chilkat inlet near its confluence with the Lynn Canal south of Haines. The milky-green water is glacial runoff. *Right:* Expert craftsmanship is depicted in Indian wood carving on display at Alaska State Museum, Juneau. A totem pole is a document carved in wood. Without a written language, Indians devised this way to record a family heritage.

Below: Spruce trees winning the fight for survival along a rocky shore of Prince of Wales Island. *Right:* Iced Salmon prior to processing by deft hands of cannery personnel in Ketchikan. Ketchikan, 695 miles north of Seattle, has been important fishing center since 1880's.

Below: Inactive gold mine within walking distance of Juneau. Viewed from Perseverance Gold Mine Trail. *Right:* Memorial lighthouse, vital aid to navigation, on the inside passage between Prince Rupert and Ketchikan.

Below: Onion-shaped domes dominate Russian Orthodox Church erected by Alexander Baranof in Kodiak. *Right:* Units of the Distant Early Warning System (DEW) on the line near Cape Simpson. This highly refined electronic system extends from the Aleutians up and along Arctic Ocean to Baffin Island, Greenland and Iceland.

Below: Gillnet fishing boats at the mouth of the Naknek River near its entry into Bristol Bay. *Right:* Early morning sun highlights commercial fishing fleet moored in a snug harbor at Cordova on Prince William Sound.

Below: View to south from a plateau near the Denali Highway, early morning sun intensifies the tremendous beauty of Mt. McKinley rising to an altitude of 20,320 feet. It is the highest point on the North American Continent which the natives called Denali "the Big One." It is the main spectacle in Mt. McKinley National Park embracing nearly 2,000,000 acres. *Right:* Beautiful red and white fox pelts drying near village on Nelson Island destined for a world famous fur market in Anchorage.

Below: Steel tower stands above enclosure protecting Prudhoe Bay oil drilling crews on frozen Arctic slope. Escaping steam is from heating system necessary for survival where temperatures may reach 70° below zero. *Right:* Stretching west from the Canadian border, massive peaks of the Brooks Range. Arctic Alaska is dominated by this largely unexplored range of mountains.

Below: King Salmon on cannery dock. Fishermen reap rich harvest of fish in many coastal waters of this vast state. *Right:* Commercial fishing boats cluster around cannery dock in Uyak Bay on west coast of Kodiak Island.

Below: Birch trees frame view from Earthquake Park up Cook Inlet. In distance downtown skyline of Anchorage, Alaska's largest city. *Right:* Massive chunks of ice afloat in Portage Lake about 2 miles long and 1 mile wide. In the background, Portage Glacier ends abruptly at water's edge. Before lake formed, glacier was used as a portage between Cook Inlet and Prince William Sound.

Below: A moose grazing leisurely in the foothills of the Nutzotin Mountains near Northway. *Right:* Tributary of the Ukak River gushes over black volcanic shale in Katmai National Monument. Situated in the southern end of the Aleutian Range, it covers an area of 2,697,590 acres.

Below: A lonesome birch lost the struggle for survival south of Kodiak above the shores of Chiniak Bay. *Right:* Evening sunlight shimmers across the mud flats of Cook Inlet at low tide near Anchorage. High tides will sometimes reach 36 feet in this area; average is 20 feet.

Below: A lonely island in the Behm Canal northeast of Ketchikan. *Right:* Mendenhall Glacier below the crest of the Mendenhall Towers lies within bulging expanse of Juneau Icecap. Icefield covers area of 1500 square miles.

Below: Looking west across a broad expanse of Tongass National Forest. Our largest national forest covers 16,000,000 acres. In the distance, peaks on Prince of Wales Island. *Right:* Torrent of water spills over rocky ledge along west coast of Prince of Wales Island at Waterfall.

Below: Icy glacier flowing through the peaks of the Chilkat Range. The deep ridges on this serrated surface will vary from a few inches to many feet in width. *Right:* Lake shore near Auke Bay north of Juneau provides protective shelter for privately-owned amphibious plane.

Below: A true Eskimo girl reflects the full beauty of youth in her colorful fur lined parka. *Right:* Coastal headlands meet icebound Bering Sea on Nelson Island.

Below: Kayak and fox pelts on drying rack silhouetted against an evening sunset on Nelson Island. Viewed within an Eskimo village on the icebound shore of the Bering Sea. *Right:* Winter ice jams form grotesque patterns on the surface of the Bering Sea south of the city of Nome. This area is almost due north of Hawaiian Islands, about the same latitude as Trondheim, Norway.

Below: Drifts of snow and ice near shore of Arctic Ocean at Prudhoe Bay. *Right:* Eskimo peers over the icy Bering Strait, perhaps the same place his forefathers traveled over the land bridge thousands of years earlier.

Below: Looking north from the rock laden shore of Porcupine Island across a broad expanse of Iliamna Lake. Approximately 80 miles in length, its eastern edge adjoins the west slope of the Aleutian Range. Literally millions of salmon enter this enormous body of water via the Kvichak River bound to their spawning grounds each year. *Right:* Arctic tundra and thousands of small lakes create an interesting pattern in summer on the Seward Peninsula. View looking north toward Council.

Below: Spruce trees encrusted with snow in the Chugach Mountains east of Anchorage. *Right:* Gold miners retreat amidst remnants of winter snow near Palmer Creek on towering hills south of Turnagain Arm.

Below: A young lead dog rests during the day near Eagle River north of Anchorage. Dogs run best at below zero temperatures and nearly all teams are now owned for pleasure or by professional trainers. *Right:* Skiers enjoy snow-covered slopes of Mt. Alyeska east of Anchorage.

Below: A weathered spruce seems determined to survive on slopes of Chugach mountains west of Copper River. *Right:* A stand of birch and spruce lends contrast to rugged peaks of the Chugach Range above Knik Arm.

Below: Fishermen ascend a gentle slope along the shore of picturesque Copper River near Chitina. In background, Chugach Mountains. *Right:* Fish drying beside smokehouse in village of Port Graham on southern tip of Kenai Peninsula. Boardwalks are common in village.

Below: Amphibious craft along the shore of Lake Spenard adjacent to the International Airport in Anchorage. *Right:* Low hanging clouds envelop the towering mountains that seemingly surround Seward. The city was named for William H. Seward, U. S. Secretary of State, who negotiated for the purchase of Alaska at a cost of $7,200,000. In foreground, Resurrection Bay.

Below: Lichen, moss, and harebell adapt to rock wall rising from the shore of Resurrection Bay near Seward. *Right:* Ribbonlike Klehini River at the base of the Chilkat Range, viewed from the lowlands northwest of Haines.

Below: Icy cold stream below Worthington Glacier near Thompson Pass north of Valdez. *Right:* Spruce cones; dense groves cover thousands of acres of coastal slopes.

Below: City of Cordova on shore of Prince William Sound at base of Eccles Mountain. This picturesque coastal community without road connection still retains an aura of old Alaska. *Right:* Granite Creek surges through rock walls on northern end of Kenai Peninsula.

Below: The Ptarmigan, Alaska's plump state bird seen in many areas. Member of the Grouse family, it turns from brown to snowy white in winter. *Right:* Yellow pond lily often seen on the many lakes and ponds in southeast and south central Alaska. Moose value them as food.

Below: The Native Store in Tununak seems determined to withstand another onslaught from an Arctic winter. Right: Sub-zero temperature is evident during a winter blizzard in the village of Tununak. To see your own feet is sometimes difficult. Eskimo people have managed to adapt their lives to this harsh, demanding environment.

Below: Polygonal grids create an interesting pattern on a carpet of tundra east of the Colville River on the shore of the Arctic Ocean. This occurrence evolves from freezing and thawing of the soil. *Right:* Wind-frayed flags supplant the yellow line to direct vehicle drivers on the Arctic slope. Visibility is near zero during winter storms.

Below: Wind carved snow and ice dominate the rocky shores of Etolin Strait in the Kuskokwim Delta. *Right:* Setting sun reflects its brilliant color on icy surface of the Bering Sea. On horizon a mail plane swings around Cape Vancouver on western edge of Nelson Island.

Below: Remains of the Council City and Solomon River Railroad at rest on a coastal plain near Solomon on the Seward Peninsula. This rail system was abandoned before being placed in operation. *Right:* The community of Bethel beside the frozen Kuskokwim River. The temperature this day was a frigid 30 degrees below zero.

Below: Blooms of poppies harken arrival of spring by aged home near Fairbanks. *Right:* Pipe in storage at Prudhoe Bay destined to carry oil from the Arctic slope to the Port of Valdez on Prince William Sound. This 48″ diameter pipeline will cover approximately 800 miles.

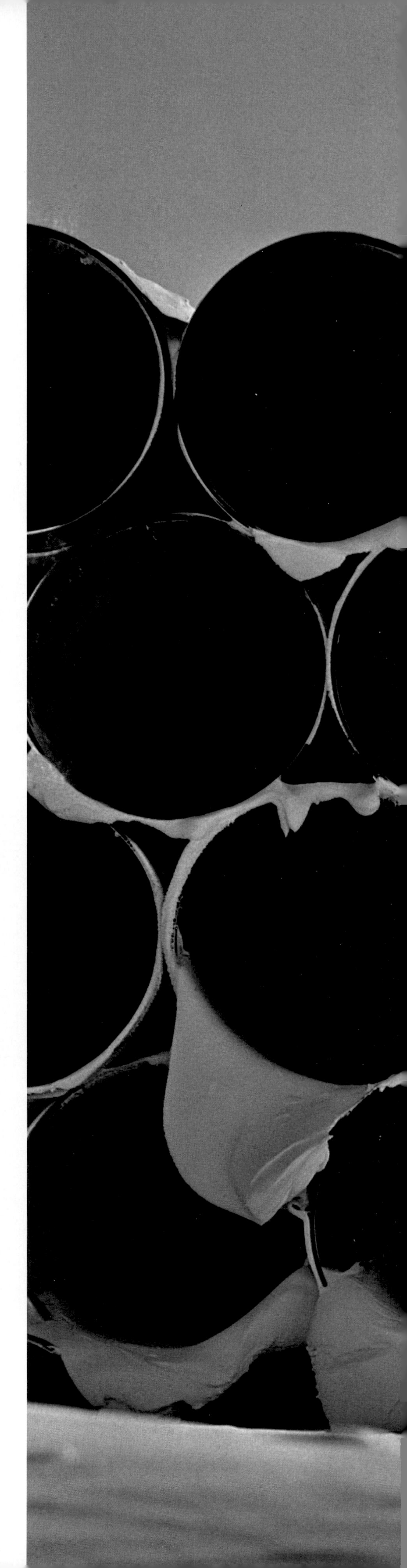

Below: Icy glaciers flow around peaks of Chilkat Range east of Glacier Bay National Monument. Dark streaks are deposits of rock and soil (moraines). *Right:* Spruce trees depict life and death on Baranof Island near Sitka.

Below: Charter plane arriving at floating dock in Waterfall on Prince of Wales Island. *Right:* Town of Ketchikan clings to base of Deer Mountain on the western edge of Revillagigedo Island. In foreground, log rafts afloat in Tongass Narrows destined for a nearby lumber mill.

Below: Early morning fog rises from the foothills of the coast mountains along Lynn Canal midway between Juneau and Haines. *Right:* Granite mountains partially covered with spruce trees slope to the shore of scenic Rudyard Bay on the Behm Canal northeast of Ketchikan.

Below: Erosion carved wall of volcanic tuff in the Valley of Ten Thousand Smokes, Katmai National Monument. Mt. Katmai erupted in 1912. *Right:* Fissured volcanic field at the base of Mt. Movarupta in Katmai National Monument. This monument was established in 1918.

Below: Massive chunks of ice ever shifting and settling along the shores of Turnagain arm. Tides up to 36 feet in height are responsible for this change. *Right:* Spruce tree reflections on the mirror-like surface of a pool in the foothills of the Chugach Mountains near Tonsina.

Below: Newly developed valley pasture along the Edgerton Highway near Lower Tonsina. In the background, foothills of the Chugach Mountains northside. *Right:* Spectacular Liberty Falls before it makes its entry into the Copper River paralleling the Edgerton Highway.

Below: Chugach Mountains reflected on mirror-like surface of melting waters of Valdez Glacier. In 1897 this glacier was used as a trail to the gold fields of the interior. *Right:* Looking south across Kachemak Bay on the Kenai Peninsula. Background, the Kenai Mountains.

Below: Weather-bleached store in Chitina appears structurally sound in this valley region. *Right:* View looking south near Northway to the Wrangell Mountains. Dense forests of birch sprinkled with spruce cover this broad rolling plain. In near foreground, the Nabesna River.

Below: Fish drying racks and snowsled in summer storage in Wainwright on the shore of the Arctic Ocean below Pt. Barrow. *Right:* Gillnet fishing boats at rest in Bristol Bay. During the salmon runs in July the fishermen and canneries operate on a twenty-four hour schedule.

Below: Salmon filets drying before entry into smokehouse at native fish camp on Tanana River. *Right:* Huge weatherworn gold-seeking dredge that once digested rocks and earth afloat in self-made lake near Nome.

Below: A waterfall on the eastern slope of Mt. Juneau above Perseverance Gold Mine Trail. In foreground, birch trees are adorned with rich green of spring. *Right:* Aerial view of an Alaska State Ferry sailing north along the inside passage near Ketchikan. Ice-free the year around, waterways of southeast Alaska are rich in the beauties of waterfalls, fjords and snow-packed glaciers.

Below: Brilliant sun highlights oil derrick (height 150 feet) near Prudhoe Bay on the Arctic slope. Drilling pipe is handled from the topman house attached to side of derrick. It pierces the earth to a depth of nearly 10,000 feet where it enters a production reservoir. Permafrost in this region will vary from 1900 to 2200 feet deep. *Right:* On the western edge of Nelson Island, Eskimos prepare to move supplies back to their nearby village.

Below: Late evening sun reflection on planes beside landing strip in Kotzebue. Foreground, natives await the arrival of incoming plane. *Right:* Low hanging clouds frequently envelop portions of the ice worn peaks in Mt. McKinley National Park. Foreground, brushy tundra.

Below: Russian Orthodox chapel on the Kenai Peninsula overlooking Cook Inlet. This chapel established in 1846 is typical of Russian church architecture in Alaska. *Right:* Rocky shore along the western edge of Kodiak Island ever awash from rain and sea. On horizon, northern shore of Uyak Bay near waters of Shelikof Strait.

Below: Remnants of winter snow near Thompson Pass (elevation 2,722 feet) on Richardson Highway east of Valdez. *Right:* Boulder Creek cascades over massive granite rocks prior to its entry into Chickaloon River.

Below: Majestic Mt. Iliamna (elevation 10,116 feet) on crest of the Aleutian Range. *Right:* The somber appearance of the North Slope is often broken with varying contrasts of small lakes, islands and floating ice. View looking south along the shore of the Arctic Ocean.

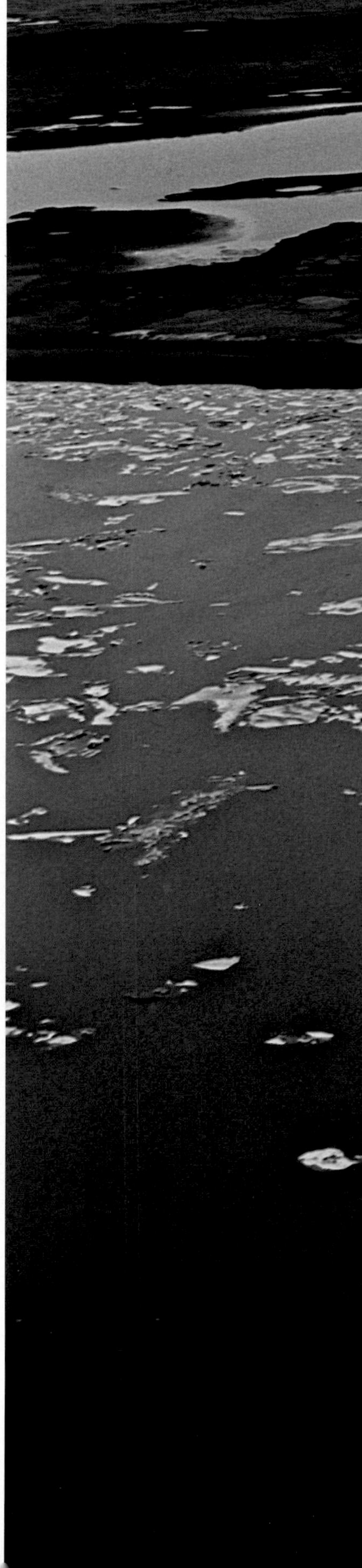

Below: Walrus hunters bound for home along the tundra covered shores of the Arctic Ocean south of Wainwright. Remnants of winter ice are still in evidence in early August. *Right:* Dense forest of birch trees along the Steese Highway. This unpaved 163 mile highway running northeastward from Fairbanks crosses Eagle Summit (elevation 3,880 feet) to Circle on Yukon River. It is literally the end of highway travel in northeast Alaska.

Below: Lonely troller appears insignificant on Stephens Passage south of Juneau. In background summit of small snow capped mountain peeks above clouds below southern tip of Glass Peninsula. *Right:* Tiny wildflowers and elfin ferns grow undisturbed in moisture laden soil.

Below: Fish wheel on the silt-filled Nenana River turns huge wire basket which scoops up unsuspecting fish as they swim upstream. Wheel is powered by river current. *Right:* Protected grave in Indian Cemetery at Eklutna along the Glenn Highway north of Anchorage. House isolates the deceased from evil spirits. In foreground, cross denotes conversion to Russian Orthodox Church.

Below: Miners cabin appears to reflect warmth and comfort north of Fairbanks near the Steese Highway. *Right:* The forests of Alaska can be unbelievably dense as evidenced by this vast stretch of recreation land north of Fairbanks. Viewed from above the Steese Highway.

Below: Moisture laden fog hangs over Mt. McKinley National Park. In foreground, dense forest of spruce rising from the edge of the Teklanika River. Right: The Snake River in Nome near its entry into the Bering Sea provides a secure harbor for ocean going barges. In background, native cabins seem firmly anchored on a gravel ledge which safeguards the river from the sea.

Below: Melting snow of the Chugach Mountains tumbles into Mineral Creek north of Valdez. *Right:* Naked Balsam poplars blushed with snow await the coming of Spring in Arctic Valley north of Anchorage.

Below: Mount Stroller White (elevation 5150 feet) can be dazzlingly bright in winter north of Mendenhall Glacier. Aerial view. *Right:* Pumice stones along stream near entry into Ukak River, Katmai National Monument.

Below: Eastern slope of Mt. Katolina on south end of Aleutian Range in Katmai National Monument. *Right:* Pools of water dot volcanic floor of Valley of Ten Thousand Smokes. Background, sheer wall of ash depicts unusual colors created by volcanic eruption of Mt. Katmai.

Below: Glowing autumn colors light quaking aspen east of Tok Junction on highway 2. *Right:* Immaculate Conception Catholic Church in Fairbanks established in 1904 by Father Monroe. In 1912 the populace moved church via logs across Chena River to present location.

RRINGTON CO.

Below: Snow-covered shorelines create interesting outline pattern on densely forested islands of Glacier Bay National Park. *Right:* Camera captures Tlingit Indian carving above entrance to Sitka National Monument. Northwest coast Indian wood carvings are valued highly.

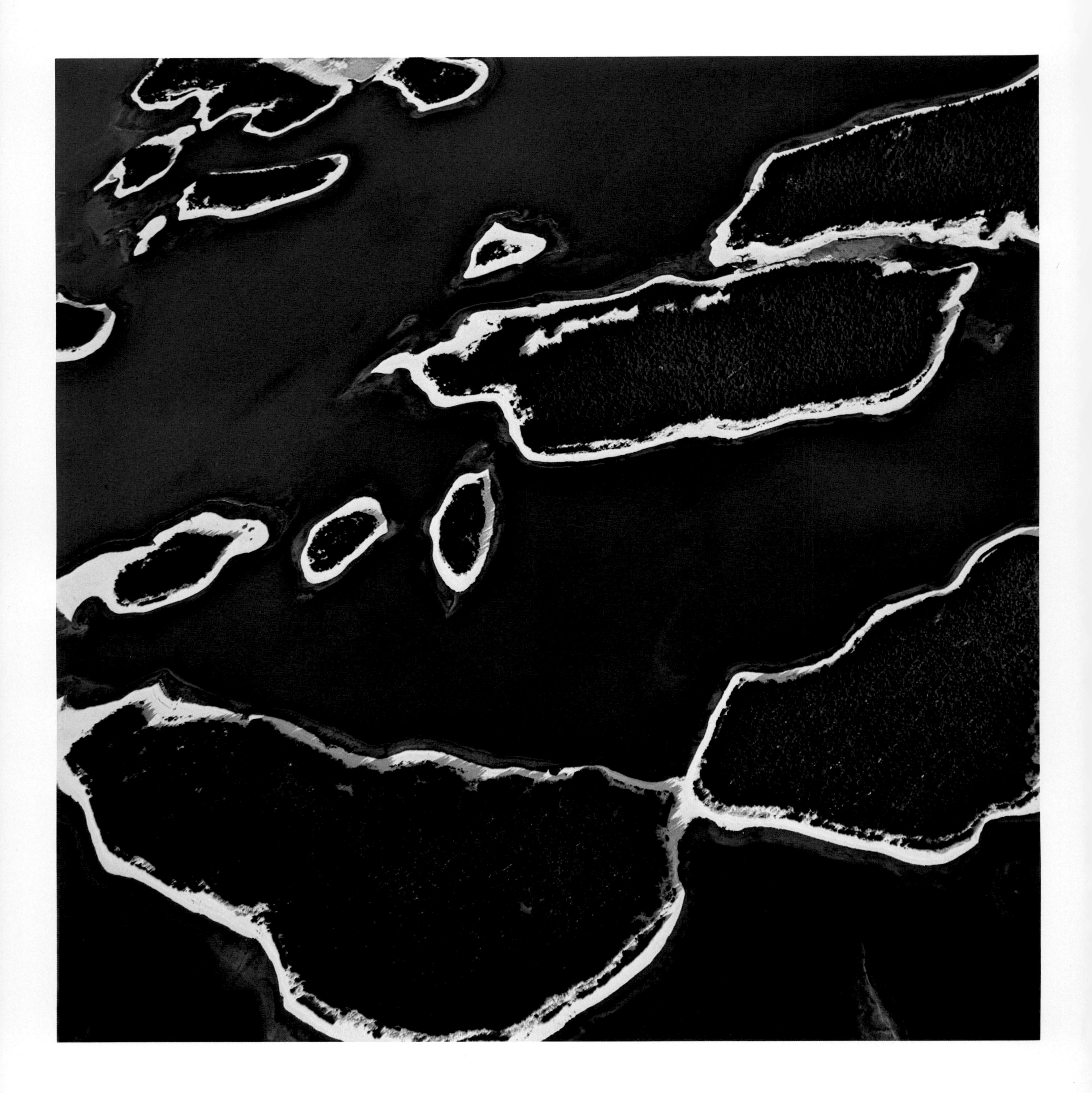

Below: Extensive tide flats near Hope render unusual contrast with the distant Chugach mountains. *Right:* Spruce trees seem determined to survive atop huge rock formation along shore of Cook Inlet near Anchorage.